Diony Chronicles

Robert Bruwer

Cyberwit.net
HIG 45 Kaushambi Kunj, Kalindipuram
Allahabad - 211011 (U.P.) India
http://www.cyberwit.net
Tel: +(91) 9415091004
E-mail: info@cyberwit.net

Printed at Repro India Limited.

Contents

Transcend the Ouroboros (Escape the Matrix)

(i)
samadhi poetry strikes the invisible target
labeled niche today as pearls with swine waste away.
lines of tigers-eye crystal sunsets
setting on a sleeping city
until time catches up
rising with a martini & a cross in between candles
'no middle way out the waste land...'

   (ii)
at the summit of Thiksey hill
east of Leh, in northern India
sits a monastery
where saffron robed monks
paint mandalas with granules of crushed
colored stone
each grain
placed to lay in the baroque shaped labyrinthine

wielding a funnel shaped
chak-pur as their surgical paint brush
several Buddhist artists
spend several weeks
dotting each microscopic
crushed & crystalized grain of pigment.
gypsum, ocher, sandstone, charcoal
corn, pollen, bark & charnel ground
orchestrated with atomic
geometric

synchronistic order.
layering hypnotic patterns
from the center outwards
before suddenly
muddling the lines
in a chaotic dismantling of their
sistine chapel-like
temple adorning artwork.

{multiplicities in process philosophy
rooted rhizomatic.ally on planes of immanence}

(iii)
welcome to the slow cancellation of the future:
a realism where
mass psychosis & nostalgia fetishism
grips the new youth
who are stalked by the zombie
dressed in mass produced parasitical polyester
whispering abstract fiat verse
as they cast a curse on Gaia
and on those
born across the tracks in the cracked red bricks

(iv)
lost pirates ((who would be at sea in the harbor of fort knox))
stepped onto paradise's shore
growing vulturous
prospector
immigrant roots
bringing alien seeds
to pillage the land
feeding the flag's mechanic furnace

exchanged for paved
parking-lot's & double-digit lane highways

the prophetic Cree Indian chief & tribe
sang & beat the drum of an axiological proverb
an ancient river & forest song
ringing true, now to our doom:
all that glitters is as abstract
a concept as the price of gold

  (v)
yesterday fades as the curtain call
fell over autumn

soaking in the apricity
my body slumped
from hours spent in the chambered
throes of Meraki

breathing in freshly brewed fika
under a lucent apricot winter sun

noise fades into harmonious music
as barking dogs, traffic & crackling static
constellate & i tessellate

opening a moleskin journal
writing on recycled notebook pages:
"bucketlists & checklists miss the view
cut to frame in front of you
                endless thumb driven scrolling
is the rope to hang you"

earthworms & beavers

are the artisans to rebuild the mud & timber
onyx tower of tomorrow
out of Babel's dust & ash
among a fossilized species
plagued by a Jehovah-complex
built on a sandy soil podium
solely for placing first
playing schizophrenic games
with linguistics & semiotics

 (vi)
invisible shackles of the mind
bind all born into the tribe of blood,
flesh & bone

cut the chains by guillotine
to lines of reggae emancipation

escape the realm
ruled by the matrix throne
        transcend beyond the ouroboros

reflections in the chapel of sacred mirrors

goddess of the celestial halls behind my eyes
who wears the rainbow as a cloak
and maps intergalactic terrains within me

Satyrs dance on the vaporous misty stairs
peeling the veil of synesthesia
to reveal a vanilla scented pan flute forrest
where clocks stand still for months to dissolve in a wink

telepathic machine elves step out from the shadows
bouncing in tangerine and turquoise gabardine's
offering silent secrets of holographic dimensions
where fragments all fuse into holistic singularity

handing me a cedar Midas-touched brush
before vanishing back into their black brane realm
hanging over the sky and down through the ground
on strings impenetrable by light & invisible to uninitiated eyes

transcendental transmissions cascade through me
fragmented constellations stream in luminous waves
emerging out of my vessel onto the canvas
with coalescent brush strokes in a full-bodied paint storm

the chapel of sacred mirrors shimmers
on the shore of springs undying ocean
under the dome where the apricot sun beams
feeding the flowering greenery rolling on ancient hills

ancestral voices whisper a spellbinding mantra
painting a coup de maître in sleeps dream kingdom
with hypnotic hallucination activating frequencies
i melt into the cosmic incense smoke pools of stardust

The Age of Alienation [& other poems by the 'Book Burning, Gun Slinging Society']

i.
  on the eve of the beginning
we swam in the vast nothingness of an eternal now
spellbound in the sea of retrograde amnesia

born into a plague
& primed by spacetime abstractions
ripped out of childlike purity
& morphed into a disfigured automaton species

stalking the asphalt planes of the panopticon
with heads hung by the burden of dim lit distractions
tailored for the livestock subscribed
to the web shaped shackles

at the foot of life's lonely mountain
the summit appears to rise & disappear
  unscalable the snowcaps melts into the heavens

ii.
  mapping the blank trackless pages
on my own odyssey
- a journey of expanding cartography
in the desolate wilderness of poetry & 21st century philosophy
- beyond the walls & platonic disfigured forms
my scourge is housebound
periodic slants in discourtesy by my menage
  "im yirtzeh hashem".

a classic case of family tree suffering -
struck by a bout of root rot.

deep sigh in
mantra
slow sigh out
mechanical cogs act as dials
on the dashboard of perception
yet the observer lies unbound
in the realm of the transcendental

iii.
staring out the window
watching birds flutter in a mating dance
my gaze
collapses
drifting out of the frame & into an internal debate
to which i'm a spectator?
are we three, i wonder...
both participant(s) & mediator in the puzzling di(tri)alogue
centered on 'for' & 'against' a trip to the barber for a haircut
while the voices ramble on inside my fragmented mind
i let my attention step outside
taking flight with the dirty dancing budgies
running my hand though my hair
turning cold
what if i start balding?

on a seesaw swaying from
'greatest hit haircuts' highlight reels
to visions of the shiniest chrome dome in the city
lost...
blooming sunny weather
lost...

iv.
both long-hand & short-hand
revolve in an infinite circuit

high-brow & low-brow
hands all pointed at the gyrating face

who is the author of my dreams
& he who visits me when i am engulfed
by the busy swarm of creativity

mystical genie who appears from his cave
shaping syllables & words
out of the buzzing humdrum
clear as black ink on a white page...
it streams out of my hand
at a rate which i cling to
as i am whisked through
that flower garden of poetry

v.
    Q. answer Fermi's paradox ::

~ we are the aliens

Dimethyltryptamine Daydream

Orphan Ontology (an obituary for father time & mother earth)

swap the snapping turtles for shadow puppets
it's Plato's cave all the way down

shimmering hexagonal revelations
stream through my Dimethyltryptamine daydream

out of my eyes unfurled the room
& then the world was birthed from my womb

faint as a whisper, yet haunting
a spectre lingers in the ether
heavy charcoal clouds hanging over me

under orange smoke, I pray
in dusty days of this drought-stricken
Eleusinian mystery
where the flowers which you painted in the spring
have turned a pale shade of grey disarray

a black hole sun hovers where the superlunary
ought to be
& i find myself lost with insomnia
seeking aletheia on a polar night
stumbling around the thorny maze of my own creation
in the tattered pair of shoes
painted by Vincent van Gogh

in that little ice age
Nietzsche's demon spoke the cursed words
spelling out my Sisyphean eternal recurrence
to carry an acacia cyclops cross
sprawled across the breadth of my back
crafted by my clumsy hands
splintered & bloody as they deserve to be
for letting you slip through
when my skies were still blue

le masochiste

mouth to mouth
breathing in sweet morphine
she's analgesic

fill my lungs
with toxin antihistamine
kiss me quick
kill the seeds of sick

unwinding me
unraveling at the seams
a knitting needle
piercing through my skin

jinx one-two twice
junk found on a spoon
shot up flooding veins
leads to a fork
at yellow-brick roads untraveled

reshuffle the deck of playing cards
draw another hand
the house has me stoned & frozen
sinking deeper into the sand

steepled fingers

tip-toe through a church temple
burn, burn, burn the system
  and bring down the cathedral

cats chase paper airplanes
along smoke
         and mirror laced red carpet trails
meeting where butterflies play
    symmetry games
     en route to cemetery gates

ೇ ೇ ೇ ೇ
Justine sang the libertine song
marching with Marquis de Sade
in boots of Spanish leather
across a whip-scarred back of a hostage
in rain soaked Stockholm
begging in quivering seesaw voice
    'please sir,
       hold me closely
          & let me leave'

la•petite•mort

let me kiss you
below the depths
touched by simmering rays
crashing like waves onto your bronzing skin
on a sunny day
may ravenous fangs
sink into the nape of your neck
holding back the pining force
of seven hundred clamping bear-traps
starving to death for your tomb of life
    la petit mort // la petit mort
an afterlife womb
  where heaven & hell mix
      craving more & more
gliding fingers ski southward
tracing outlines along silky snow
   i connect freckles
                dot•to•dot
sketching a finger-painted masterpiece
along the canvas of your burning flesh
hallelujah
hallelujah

hips thrust up as lips meet lips
now dissolve on my tongue

shifting gears & counting speed
melting me as she breathes
earthquakes shake over•quivering bodies

turning calm seas into wild stormy high tides
blood rushes into flushed cheeks
she floods my shore
like a tsunami at the break of dawn
on all fours begging for more
black on white strikes gold
while grey melts in between
tap-tap the beat of a snare drum
hitting the high hats where the dots of i
meet the passing crossroads of u6s6
sweet & sour sweat drips
splashing from sheets onto the floor
steam sways & burns
as the scent of burning wood
fills the empty spaces of our room
an unspoken language with signs of smoke
as flames burn through the old
& come again glimmering new

((Dante themed, Dylan styled)) Protest Song

Arthur Schopenhauer //
> *for where did Dante take the material of his hell*
but from our actual world?

shut up, sit down
write & recite the rules
          line up, melt down
snowflakes re*shaped* for tools
bright eyed sandpit artisans
crushed under thumb
shaped to retrograde
& handmade into a-grade wage slaves
set for a cubicle daze till coffin days.
god bless the progress
of fetish dressed
uniform boys & girls in prison shaped schools
pop goes the panopticon.
lock up, kneel down
shots ring out
one, two
another shooter burst through the gates

rinse & repeat smells like insanity
polluted streams led fish to climb trees
set in the garden of eden
where men of the cloak
hand out bonus points to kids on their knees
in classrooms
built for stealing human nature

pipe down, pipe down the throat
time for the force feeding
of alienation indoctrination
& fat duck consumer propaganda
turn to the closing page & a menu of foie gras
lays in wait for graduated waiters later
climb the snake laden ladder
where the rats race for fat cats
'on your marx'
head on the chopping block
retrenched & savings lost by suit & tie
gambling men on the stock market

    Segui il tuo corso, e lascia dir le genti

tea time, turning tide
lead the banking thieves to the guillotine

game face, cut chains
workers unite & paint the town red tonight

bail out this & burn in hell as the system falls
a new future is to be born with the rising dawn

these mountains echo the last kalahari bush-man song

ese mountains echo the last kalahari bushman song ::
:: a shaman story on the birth of art & consciousness

rhythmically I moved
stomping in a circular dance
clapping my hands & slapping my thighs
clicking my tongue & chanting low humming tones
slipping in & out of a hologram dissolving trance
with a forceful energy
inexplicably electric within me
considering my five day fast preceding
only broken by rubbing Hoodai cactus gel
on my gums & chewing on Buchu leaves

ti Àkhats ta Âna Âgao?

I took flight in the camel thorn bonfire smoke
rising out from the cauldron of boiling noru noru tea
drawn from root bulbs of the ferraria glutinosa flowering stems
& with a thick layer of eland & kudu fat
smeared on my forehead, forearms & shins
I soared above the dunes of the Kalahari desert
my closed eyes mesmerised
by the yellow devil thorn flowers
melting into honeycomb shaped
geometric chevrons & vortices

!gâi daoba ûhâ re

after a dozen hours the ravenous fire within my belly
began to smolder into a dying ember
& my flight traversing realms of the dead & unborn
animal, alien, half-human & all life forms in between
began descending before landing in a narrow tunnel
within the Drakensberg mountains
where my transformation
into a herbal medicine man was complete
in that cradle of mankind
reborn
I came to be an interdimensional
shape shifting shaman
eternally

!gui gowa-i ge tatse Ââusa tama hâ

painted rock face cave walls retell the origin story
paired with the transcendent ability
to share & pass down intergenerational history
using the vast vices of art
  those mountains echo the birth of consciousness
a cyclical fairytale of suffering
known as the human condition

Combustion & Creation (portrait of a para-noid artist, smoking)

midnight disease :: a journey with hypergraphia

life arrived with a birthmark
burnt by the touch of a daemon shaped flame
  leading the artist down a lifelong maze
only guided by the scorching Promethean torch
along the anointed namesake road
    which delves into & through shadows
to dwell in that ethereal realm
    vaporous as floating smoke from the cigarette tip
blown in a cloud before dissolving
into an unknown dimension

with eyes which sway like a ship on stormy waves
side to side long after day sets
the mind is never dismissed to rest.
repeated invasive visions ransack his idle hands
where he awakes as the prodigal son
shouting prayers in barren exile
he pleads ::
              erect a stoa, built with my bones
at the crossroads where east & west meet.
        streaming rows of ultraviolet light
guide magi & horsemen alike
stripping the scales
clean off of their blind, blinkered, wandering eyes

& the mantra hangs the sun
to stay overhead for a Joshua fashioned day
& delay darkness of nightfall
evermore

ghosts of my life (sinking in a stream of consciousness)

ACT 1
MELTING into the crucible
of her sapphire and steel stare
i felt myself turn into liquid
in the most lucid fluid stream
where my outlines disappeared
with my insides dispersed on the table of a roadside cafe
plucked out of the nineteen forties.
lost in the smooth swing of background
Glen Miller big band jazz
& a chorus of old man monotone conversation
volume turning up a few bars
at an attempt in outcompeting
every rusting turn of crinkled
secondhand newspaper page.
hunters, soldiers, tailors & painters
seemed to account for the patronage
as this fever-dream slipped deeper
into the uncanny valley of out-of-place strange
only for my surreal thoughts (a mirror of perception)
to jolt back into this distant reality
  as an elderly woman dressed in wartime threads
started shouting 'this is a trap
    we are in the void of nothingness.'
i jumped, throwing the contents of my wallet
paper & metal onto the table & in brisk strides
ran towards the door
exhausted by the entire diner scene

best described as the entanglement
of Edward Hopper smashed
into Rene Magritte
within the Hadron Collider.

   ACT 2
LYING on his back in the lecturing hall
with powdered speed running through his veins
& the bass of jungle drumming in his ears
        rousing an hypnotic dizzying of fanged noumena

our Nietzsche launched off of the Icarus runway
rocketing headlong towards the sun
       too soon.. too young
burnt up into a crust before he fell
crashing down on beige coat land

rising beyond a falling dusk
      the owl of Minerva
spreads Athenas wings in apricot shades
    hooray the veil of grey is torn through
& the eyesore tones are washed away

facing an empty fridge
while scrounging around for a meal
will the rolling stone find freedom down the hill
  as the blonde ghost drifts off to sleep

   ACT 3
UNDER the blooming shades of sweet lemon wax
floating along a wake of seagulls
  as waves crashed into a glistening shore
before the alabaster spume was drawn with the tide

sinking, alongside my final breath
beyond the horizon
& below the bottomless depths of an ocean
too vast for the rediscovery of that gold
cast asunder
          lost overboard
on our voyage, embarked at neoliberal hell
docking in an asylum bingo hall
   stepping onto the jetty, i felt the weight
                              heart plundered
        setting off the motion for my ewige wiederkunft
                         sinking...

The Face of Murder

1. *et ignotas animum dimittit in artes*

you & I read the puzzling pages
where Zeno tore the fabric of our pink paper brains
& within that spookiness of waves & particles
in silence, we shattered as billiard balls
after the breaking dawn of timeless days

falling dusk saw the owl of Minerva
spread Athena's wings in apricot shades
as the grey veil of yesterday
was torn asunder & washed anew
in the thundering unveiling of shadows cast by hollow frames

i traced the footsteps of my existence
along countless newspaper article lines
only to find that i had been blind.
a test-tube baby born & raised in Plato's cave
where my gaze had been hypnotized by shadow puppets
    mesmerized by cheap tricks
& victim of the military industry's projectile gimmicks
facing eviction into perpetual neoliberal hell
with groundhog Minsky moment's

2. *entfreimdung*

looking up at the clouds
contemplating death & Irish airmen
as i lay on my back in a dusty paddock

where cattle once roamed
before being sent to the slaughter
    when suddenly i was yanked back into reality
with a violent urgency
demanding that i disclose the price of fish.
my internal integration turned schizophrenic
  asking 'what the price per head
to attend the sermon on mount Beatitudes could have been
  & were the fish locally caught in the lake of Galilee?'
the only certainty
was that Adam Smith baked the bread
infecting the loaves with leprosy.

3.   *la divina commedia // la vita nuova*

the sapphire eyes of the children of men
turn to a cold, hard steel
their zig-zag skipping & hopscotch dancing
shifted into stiff, uniformed
rhythmic marching by de rigueur
as a segment of the fragmented
groundhog daze

amphetamine pills melt smiles
like a urine soaked water-color painting
the playground artists are shackled by forms
& straightjacket classrooms
designed for a caged parrot
instead of a songbird with an amputated larynx

turning & turning has turned to
scrolling & scrolling in an ever narrowing gyre
with the second coming delayed

for a worthy people when pharisees
see the setting sun & burn in the fire of their making

the long-hand & short-hand revolve in an infinite circuit
there are high-brow & low-brow hands
all pointed at the gyrating face of the weeping Jeremiah

we have killed god & will do it
over & over again
until the end

Peyote Flavored Fables

after a pint of cactus laced eggnog
    i closed my eyes in time
for the creation of an in-house Christmas production

  Pt.1
The egg-yolk dawn finds me on a stingray shore
      inside an oyster cave
  my sleep stolen by tumble dryer waves
& a seashell orchestra

I weathered the snail-paced night
    under starless ceiling
  a deep onyx sky melting into the waves
I paced the beach
  covering every grain of scorching sand
picturing your body blanketing over me

  Pt.2
engraved on a sandstone slab
at the crossroads of four corners
   " *the sun will rise in the west*
        above the sandy shores of Venice
            with the reincarnation of Adonis..."

buy a ticket
    pass through cemetery gates
                & slip inside the backdoor
into the round house of flaming horrors

once your realize this is a madhouse
the holographic matrix begins falling into place

shake some peyote popcorn
& shake to shaman popsongs
under big brother's bulging eyes
out of the skull of reptilian overlords

Poseidon sings his sheepish
                                seahorse song
rocking in waves against the raft of sleep
drifting across that dreamscape ocean
flickering into ash & melted wax
of a candle burning at both poles

  Pt.3
while shouting 'look diamonds.
a floor of diamonds'
as she danced on a pile of broken glass
wearing a nylon & plasticine replica Thalia mask
stitched & glued in a factory overseas
with nets hung as a moat
outside the fifth floor window

tip-toe pirouette's
followed by a blood soaked footprint path
  she carried the paper plates
stacked with a pile of hardwood & insulation foam
before calling the piggies 'grubs up.
freshly nicked honeycomb'

Pt.4
the sun streamed through
winter green leaves
in beams of radiant light
speaking to me as a flickering flame
enchants a giant moth

clock arms bound in slings
on this crisp December morning
with birds chirp
singing songs of longing

 coral snakes choke eagles
& worms bite their own tails

> *eternally...*

black squares & circles
paint satirical gibberish
on the nonsensical left hemisphere'd canvas

turtleneck lifejackets
hung with weight of fools gold
i'm drowning in the deep end
of a pool smothered in smoke

Preludes

*

step into the shadows & embrace mystery
for a pot of gold is Stygian in a dark cave
            ...jump...
                        or take my place
standing in alienation as i trace
        the journey of the magi
at the cost of swapping the map for fertile land
  staring at a skull sized globe
in the sweltering heat of arid sub-saharan Africa
  plotting a pilgrimage in the cloudy space
within my head

**

glimmering astral bodies
        explode into light
night after night -
  a sight which led to deification by hunter-gather
ancestral aboriginal stargazers
who built monoliths in celebration of the starry maze
  each sun-dried clay tablet set in replicating place

***

a whale would have to swallow me
before i swallow my self conscious imposter syndrome
& set on the road to Nineveh
yet i ponder in child-like wonder
        is a white whale a whale?

****

the blind ontological outlook of humanism
sucks the entirety of my empathy
out of my frail body
for those poor eyes which have looked up
at the vast cosmic spread upon the ceiling of a cloudless night
  / perhaps then an asteroid of realization
would smack them in the face
knocking them off of their 'pedestal of creation'

today the horizon is a vast wasteland
painted grey
replacing the flora kingdom
                reflecting shades & tones
        stretching beyond our limited ocular spectrum
which once grew wild

*****

in the pearly silver moonlight
i exhale a rich ring of cigarette smoke
the words of Mahatma Gandhi
serving as a midnight snack of contemplation
& heavy, steely company...
                Jesus died for all
// his followers wage war
        denying refuge for the meek
turning the other cheek as plastic dinghies capsize
& children drown in the Mediterranean sea

flicking the extinguished cigarette butt
into an overflowing rubbish bin
 nodding slightly
in a spontaneous commemoration ceremony

for the last Samaritan
    forgotten are his good deeds
             while he lies deceased
eternally distressed

A Kôan [the limitations of language : on the bluntness of humanities sharpest tool]

linguistic cunnilingus as the emergence of furor poeticus
  :: out of phonetic oral sex comes lyrical transcendence

/

acacia thorns pierce the skin
while shittim pierces the veil of the perceivable
as golden incense weaves across the sky
to a sanctuary where we unwind space & time

prophet's write of the vapor turning on lights
and horns shining in rays of synesthesia

magi mixed herbs under the desert moon
which mapped a path through golden the sand

bundle's of wild harmel wood burns
as sparks flicker & dance with stars
in a moon reaching bonfire

under autumn shadows
in the harmonic hum of the aboriginal didgeridoo
drifting on the streams of wattle-seed smoke
  gazing down as the earth unfolds and refolds
        in a cymatic origami cardtrick

out of the soil grows the ship
which flies above the starry skies
fruit of biblical implications

with seeds of knowledge
& keys to ghostly dimensions

    //
Thomas Aquinas
& Meister Eikhart shared the same eye
as you & I
peel wide the smokescreen
& spy through the looking-glass used by god
  which saw god
which was the eye through which the son of god saw
& wept at the stale state
  of the collective unconscious bots
lost in spirals of consumption & mirror reflection masturbation

this is not the godless wasteland
advertised by the screaming anchormen
    fear-mongers & alarmists
who sell panic by the gallon

with electrodes probing their temporal lobes
the prophets & shaman's
are in the asylums
labeled as schizo's for their visions of angels
& demons
& messages from the god's

an amnesiac species
chasing the neurochemical highs
shaped by evolutionary design
as a means to survive

barrel of monkey's biologically
swinging about nuclear powered technology
    alienated
that far removed from nature (forest. desert. ocean)
planning to leave the planet entirely

    Om Mani Padme Hung
    OM
    Om Mani Padme Hung
    OM

dreams + psychedelic drugs as inter~dimensional portals

i dissolved as a dandelion in the eye of a tornado
on a night dimly lit up by the fading
  waning gibbous moon

wiping the scales from my eyes
  i woke up
untangling my limbs
    out of the mycelium web
spun in a kaleidoscopic razor-wire thread
winding spirals of psychedelic bungee cables
within the walls of my exploding head

a prefrontal lobe c-section
made me see the plasticity of reality
    stirring the tides of all seven thousand seas
  rising with techno-junkie tsunami rave waves
splashing onto Goa's shore with tie-dyed
  Buddhist appropriation

spinning in a drowsy trip
with hundreds of tabs open in my skull's browser
  soft electric jazz music
blows over and through me
  without a single saxophone note
lifting me off the dusty floor
        to float through my mind's sky
    across the pond to New Orleans

and the stumbling drumbeat
falling off before hitting home

alien night where both mythos and logos disperse
  lost in the spiced cigarette smoke rings
and drifting daemon daydreams
where my dark fantasy lands on the train track
with bloodshot
puffy eyes and fingers crossed
  mumbling for the trolley-cart lever-puller
to divert the machine my way
    hoping that he hears
my telepathic begging
when facing his Kantian dilemma

Fridge Magnet Poetry

|.
Wave after crisis-shaped wave
crash onto the shore of the twenty-first century.
Ice caps melts & form tsunami's
as the plastic sea spills sludge
into the streets of our colossal sand castle
beach-sand cities.

Space-age machine's & color-TV's
the baby-boomers popped post (nuclear & cold) war
champagne
blasting the economy into a state of dizzying
hungover recession
& eventual comedown depression.

The emergence of scientific arrogance
cloaked in a gimmick shaded cape
enlightened the funeral service of God
& cast a shade of nihilism darker than what Nietzsche
might have ever predicted.
Quantum physics figured it out
until the light split & caused a black-out.
Entangled in a mess we have realized how we miss
the warm fire-side bliss of myth & tribal communion.

With all this devastation the heaviest burden,
the most bitter pill /
in an ever growing medicine cabinet
  (which crawls backwards into the jungle -

where nature's pharmacological seeds
                 still heal the the deepest wounds)
/ is that we exist in the time of *fridge magnet poetry.*
From biblical verse
to quantum definitions
of the material down to matters of the heart...

Romanticism strung in golden strands
through all of nature and eventually into the depths of the uncon-
scious
Studying and interpreting dreams
among the surreal mind-bending themes.

Perhaps I am the anomaly, a test tube baby
chained to the bookshelves in my old town library
Reading each line as if my eyes
were absorbing the ink through the air
as an oxygen-giving & brain-blowing tonic.

II.
Poets, mystics & philosophers
have been the creators & legislators of society
for all of recorded history
(their quills testify on those brilliant canvas paintings)
Leaving the stem sciences to mathematically
catch up when their numbers checked out.
Plato and Aristotle spoke to this fact
in the great Grecian symposiums.
Shelley penned protest verse
in divine defense of the importance.

Yeats notion'd the gyres & fundamentals
of intuition-based poetics, with the sentence wrestling

taking a backseat
smelling the sweet instinct scented roses
which Eliot wrote about in pointed prose
essay after essay of artistic assessment
of the metaphysical poets & the modern emergence...

Dare we question the machine
which invented all computing machines
& controls the functions of complex organs
pumping blood around the clock
& inhaling oxygen
before exhaling a new element
    all in independent unconscious meticulous precision.
That neuronal miracle which processes thousands of stimuli
In the blink of an eye
& sifts and sieves through the sensory sleeves
in the kingdom where our sleep meets dreams
forming the simulation we call reality.

III.
In the search for health and comfort
with surplus stacked up for doomsday
and hoarded riches
which it seems
in our greed we may squeeze through a needles eye
riding on the back of military trained camel's.
Guns & bombs & jets & nitrous mustard gases.
We have sacrificed our souls
& labeled it a mental health crisis
in the fat cat capitalist pursuit of pushing pills
until we sit in a drooling mess as a shell of the genius
our nature has evolved to shape us with.
But in this dualistic paradox

it should be suggested
that the definite certainty of physical expiration is known
but what of our souls...
The rotten pit without compassion or gratitude
our souls have gone to hell while we live in this plastic
materialist heaven.
In a limp whimper we devour the great mother
in a whimper this world will end
leaving behind the god-forsaken
fridge magnet poetry…

Meditations of a Mystic (Time is an Ocean Without a Shore)

I

if all cobblestone & volcanic tuff roads lead to Rome
then those limestone roads also leave Rome

Heraclitus wrote & wove the bridge
which stretches across aeons
rotating in orbit through Hindu Yuga seasons

empires which crossed oceans
& hoarded Maia's glistening minerals
with riches sinking to the molten core
rose at dawn before the fall
to set as the sun & new dynasties
came forth once more

II

winding & unwinding the cogs
of my mechanical mind
each molecule stretched by time
unfolding the origami within me
a transcendental mirror reflects
out of the dark room inside
bursting in light onto a paper page

i set sail guided by a star at the centre
of the poetic tradition solar system
with each stroke of the pen
a battle of egoic & stoic reflection

as a magi walking on a tightrope
across the galaxy of literary immortality
appointed vocal vessel for the ætheric genie's
anointed scribe by name only

|||

war & famine plague the flesh
while recession & depression stretch the faith
the sage & shaman among the tribe
whether congregating in concrete cities
or oak & birch tree jungles
see beyond the cage of spacetime
dancing & laughing at the gimmick false idols
which shine in pyrite light
burning out to fall of the slippery slope'd
heights set on pride

|V

animal slave to brain chemical tease
retreating into a state of frangible figurine
shaped with glass & clay hiding inside
ossified
as the kamikaze chitter chatter raid
of the autonoetic pendulum planes
rain white noise to blackout the range of color outside

cubicle-cell'd school indoctrination
where teachers spewed misinformation
of false-prophets & misconstrued tombs
to warrant imprudent cathedrals
built as astronomically aligned limestone
& dolomite megalithic calendar's & clocks
built in archer-eyed silence
yesterday

V

a voice in the sleeve-pocket
of an outside crusader
drives the night
& breaks down stable gates
spilling out onto the pavement

Athenian whispers rise out of a lamp
lighting the path of blind night
unravelling the binding rope
tied to cease the flight of shaman-like sight

scalpel c-section lobotomy
cure for epileptic seizure
stirs Manaus waters to mingle stirringly

yin yang compass paves grey to day
& mist fades on the weightless
drifting seesaw sway

three Moirai dragged Jonah
above the heavy whale tomb depths
& left him facing Shakespeare's sling & arrows
which shoot into nirvana

Morpheus points to two doors
one leads to Moriah
the other ends in Gomorrah
along which will you venture
or will you lay down to sleep
fading into to-morrow?

Portrait of the Artist as a Schizophrenic

i.
you knew me as the divo triformis
part Adonis, Apollo & Dionysus

artisan of poetic lyrical music
picture of perfect hemispheric equilibrium
            anima / animus
            mortal / celestial
taoist pendulum
                & buddhist median

now here i stand with a multiplicity of personalities
fragments of the imagined & conjured

shaman with schizophrenic rhetoric
mixture of invented mythic pseudonyms
  animal / human
mania / melancholia
    psychotic maze
& soporific daze

ii.
the sunflowers speak in my tongue
as my bee-kin buzz

rhizomatic magic
unshackled from the dysphoric capitalistic chains
  & mace chain flail whiplash
tearing my flesh apart of my inside face

in the orchid garden
with the whispering wasps
    my chest is warm
as i play with my shadows in the pollen atmosphere
of my safe space
    instead of the displaced hellscape
panopticon prison with blindingly bright
white
ten foot mirror-prism walls
    under shopping mall fluorescent lights
guarded by grey
brain whispering
shapeshifting alien demons

  iii.
barbie doll pink plastic flamingoes
stalk my daydreams
raping the silence of my private contemplation
in sacred yogic meditation
with the blood curling screeching rubber faux caw's

i fly with owls in moonlit cloud waves
in the nocturnal feasting ritual -
not the disney-meetes-anime cartoon owl
but the predator with blood
fur and mouse meat hanging
dripping off of her scalpel-sharp talons

  iv.
my punctured mind
    deflated of reality scented air
inflated by hysterical phases of aberrant salience
    as i drown under flash flood waves

of dopamine
     bursting my cranium seams
spilling me into hopscotch paranoia
               at the sound of a pin drop

i must stop....
                    this nanosecond
           each
key
typed
      has me placed under further surveillance
i am being watched by thirty three cops
  & a swat team has my laptop tapped

naughts and crosses
on the forehead wrinkles
my toes tap
when i call it tic-tac-toe

the king is a jester

in sterquiliniis invenitur

a spectre hangs over the globe
casting an everlong shadow
                from capsule thrones

grey faces glow & hang low
glued to the shimmering spectacle

hospital beds all occupied
    needles lie sidewalk to sidewalk
spreading across the line which divides
        skid-row floods the city plateau
                            tent cities spread & grow
with empty apartments counted as assets
        not homes

drone strikes burst water vessels
exploding into legless & headless children

blue planet in the dark starry cosmos
spinning in flames with a new green god
        to blame

electrical hypnotist con-artists
dabble in alchemical
            neurochemical experiments
playing Pavlovian games
with wireless airwave chained
    wage slave peasants brains

Ode to Julia (Devotion of Body, Mind and Soul)

I.
in the Mediterranean sun of Sardina
listening to the launedda pipes play
  you fed me carte de musica
topped with pecorino and fennel
while we drank a bottle
of garnet red Grenache
as the sun set
our red wine stained lips touched

nourished by a feast
which satisfied all five senses
  the durum bread and Cannonau wine
delivered life through body and blood
sending electricity
  shooting up my spine

II.
I rode alone
  along the coastal Mumbai streets
among the palm-trees and humidity
  until I reached the lush
Sivananda Ashram Yoga campus
  where the karma yogi's bowed
greeting me
  before I closed my eyes in meditation
for twelve weeks

streams gushed out of the dam
emptying my mind
  quenching the thirst deep within me
as I flowed floating along the Ganges
in the form of water
  my spirit saturated

  III.
with chakras aligned
and my third eye opened wide
I washed up on Bali beach
  crashing with fluid zen momentum
and overflowing with optimism
  while surfing the waves of Padang-Padang
  I saw her golden skin
rising out above the ocean's horizon

two year's later and married to Julia
    the mermaid who rose out of the sea
  and swam into my arms
in Indonesia

Vision #137: all the world's an asylum

dissolve me in laudanum
until my bones form a lemniscate crown
bound with a ripped & torn
      skin formed ribbon

unwrap the hand woven Ethiopian scarf
& burn the herbs found within
in a bonfire reaching above night's darkest ceiling

a specter hangs over the globe
casting an everlong shadow
          from capsule thrones

grey faces glow & hang low
glued to the shimmering spectacle

hospital beds all occupied
needles lie sidewalk to sidewalk

tent cities spread & grow
with empty apartments counted as assets
        not homes

drone strikes burst water vessels
exploding into legless & headless children

blue planet in the dark starry cosmos
spinning in flames with a new green god
      to blame

sink into black amazonian beach sand
where lithium pills are soaked in pink bleach
beneath fluorescent waves
                         & northern flashing lights

hold my hand to the edge of flowering land
where the old cloaked man croaks his speech
& I'll escape
     taking off into illuminating flight

Third Eye Wide (DMT for Free)

the eye of Horus weeps a remedy rhythmically
with the setting sun & rising moon
above waves of light & sound shrunk to a spike

midnight eye designed in amphibian days
filled with rhombohedron electric crystals
pinned at the cross point on the golden seat

sleeping eye stacked with carbonate minerals
which pave the geomagnetic maps
lining the skies of homing pigeon flight

midnight's hour peels the lid wide open
to treasure found at the summit
of the silver lined kundalini spinal ladder

in dream's kingdom atop the pinnacle
of Joseph's golden stairway to heaven
mechanical elves dance to shaman drums

in the deepest ocean of sleep
with the all-seeing eye of Horus awake
doors are unhinged & laws of time & space erased

Pardes Rimonim

~ ãÛ ~
magus of golden dawn
wielding a purpleheart-wood wand & Nandaka sword
with penchants written at the cataclysmic flood
his fire opal chalice flows with Dionysus' blood

Mercury carries the canticles
spilled from his erupting fountain pen
through the steamy air
over her breasts & up her neck into her widening ear

"let us mix & mingle our sacred liquids in that ancient
alchemical tradition
together we'll stir
the sweetest potion
elixir & spagyric mixture"

~ ˜ÔÌÔ ~
priestess of the silver star & prima materia
wearing a crown bearing luna : waxing, waning & full
with a waterfall robe to quench all thirst
& plump, bursting pomegranate fruit for his hunger

dark & light pillars from Solomon's temple
flank her left & right
while in the centre her scroll awaits his ink
to write 'Ò' (gimel) - pleasure & pain

"let us mix & mingle our sacred liquids in that ancient
alchemical tradition
together we'll stir
the sweetest potion
elixir & spagyric mixture"

Alchemy of Loveas above, from the cosmic darkness

in the collision & explosion of neutron stars
so below, within black volcanic rock
& deep underneath charcoal terra preta
the continuum is an astral phenomenon
asteroid streaks below the feet of the magi
who are guided by glimmering lamps in the night sky.

in the pomegranate garden i saw the diva triformis
with her bow, golden cloak & purple boots
the moonlight dancing in silver pools
& illuminating her ribbon strung hair
twinkling in waves of luminous æther
mingled in the air, where i swam
across the astral planes, to meet her there.

i breath in a pearl of oscillating energy
traversing curtain'd dimensions
above clouds of limited comprehension
& visceral understanding

pitcher pulled from the fountain
by the rotation of cistern wheel
overflowing golden bowl is strung
up & along the silver hung stairwell cord

Atum spoke at that frequency
seven waves of spells

crashing onto the papyrus of Ani
the sea took the coffin away that day

bird of a golden dawn
ascend on that harpsichord note
known to the father of king Solomon
who built the temple in vibration of that hum

book of the dead bound by Nile reeds
strung along with amulets
lies beneath the flight of a wing'd beast
rising out of the cadaver, i will meet her there

human shaped disaster between the stars

at the interstellar crossroads
   where the continuum is discontinued
& synthetic pulses are disconnected
   space quivers in the dusty death
of a white dwarf stars afterbirth

  there
     magicians sit playing poker
     shovelling lab farmed crisps
      into their mouths
     while dissecting nouns
pulled out of a bottomless electric hat

black-outs shadow the last farm
        held together with tofu dreg
     where gold spray painted troughs
        filled with plastic pearls
     feed the lost boys and girls
on their last wooden peg legs

 in the sway of that dark disarray
   the bay of plenty sells out
    offering discount on bluefin tuna
     & the broken body of Jesus Christ
while in the thick of the spending spree
bubonic fleas pounce from mice taxis
bending Eden to beg on knees

       20/20
clarity strikes with grandfather clock wisdom
as bells chime a revelation
ringing the proclamation song
singing
         we are the disease

High Fish and Low Eyes in Multiple Dimensions

let us go to the wire wall of lights
said the fisherman to the priest
all this chalkboard bread and tea
for bent blind wanderers to feed.
hooks and lines sink into eyes
you cloth keeps them polished dry
lakeside libraries crushed to dust
showrooms burn fluorescent nights.

desks are empty of books and pens
the priest thinly replied
cameras and microphones magnetise
strung out tight in that rope
we jumped hoops crossing fireside skies
to learn this trade
crippled cities camp out on streets
hands held up they wait.

spread across the woodland road
wolftraps lie with sugared teeth
the trees are filled with birdcage links
owls frown while bluebirds speak
shadows stalk their frames in masked silence
on the pitch black ground
a tangle box and bookmark robe
rode swiftly in
on a wind blown above pound for pound.

storm the west coast station
build a higher town

burn the gold carved tower
reclaim the fallen crown

propaganda is a hoax, to sell you insurance

streets stained with unschooled blood
washing tracks with floods of mud
ship rudders turn stuck in that sludge
olive branches sinking in tears of a dove
reruns are boring.

barroom brawls fall short of grace
vomiting the bitter taste of losing face
cut the fat cake of entitled waste
swing open the doors to pearly gates
destiny is calling.

yesterday burns a paper bonfire
mountain of ash lie serving a reminder
abstinence bites but propels even higher
poison pills paint illusions growing tired
drunk chat yawning.

wings bathed in bird seed season
crossing waltz art and foxtrot reason
stuck record songs spin unforgotten
long stale tongues reek stinking rotten
soaped mouths bubbling.

wolf shouting howls at a painted mirror
haircuts crack splitting the strongest pillar
rooster calling thrice seeking a martyr
assaulted sleeping princess stole happy after
spilled milk drying.

pill popping cats light up all nine
distillation cursed the gift of wine
rich and poor ink a wider ruled line
Tesla's pearls lying in pens with swine
gambling died trying.

toddler painting breaking the bank
shoelace whipped scars deepest crack
tortoise shells slip reversing back
sidewalk smiles hit harder than smack
hunger feeds breeding.

shades of blue out of a paint catalogue (4 days watching clouds)

(i)
silence is the seed
watered by the headbanging of blank page walls

pin prick focus
feeds the soil manure
& when these fertile elements
collide with time
the fruit echoes divine.

 (ii)
in the Eleusinian ruins
under chisel & brush
peeled pomegranate seed chambers
expose mythical relics inside chests
next to an ornament with ergot bitten dentures
& a skull painted with poppy fused inks.

in the dust lay a cracked lekythos
with traces of kykeon sediment
alongside a stitched leather satchel
filled with dried apricots & crushed nuts.

clay tablets with portraits rof priests
holding scepters & vessels
            ——— pine torches & horses adorn
those red clay ornamental sculptures.

(iii)
in a puff of cigar smoke
i was flung off of the bulls back
& impaled with the horns
of a piercing inquisitive storm
& sleep's eternal inquisition.

saturated in fields
of bohemian art & mystical philosophy
where i sat at the bench of avant garde views
marked by libertine graffiti
under chain wrapped
leather spiked straps of anarchy.

for five months
i lived in isolation
in that single bed closet of a room
without window
or television
my only view of the world outside
came from inside those ancient texts
birthing futuristic visions.

a tumbler of whisky
& single vanilla infused
tobacco cigarette
became the only indulgence
in moments of rest
with feet up & mind unbuckled.

(iv)
castle built on sand
with Velcro straps and shoelace latches

stands cracked under ram horn blown
war songs

those vibracrete walls
crest fallen by the mockery
of shepherd anthems
covered in confetti
& spray painted graffiti
        ////
for four days i watched the clouds multiply
      vapour droplets of food colouring in a bucket of water
members of a child imagined / 'eye-spy' animal kingdom
   moving through the sky in a rain hinting stampede
   *   \\\\
    on the fifth day i woke up to a chambray sky
which in the swan lake breeze reflected the cornflowers
no cloud in sight plastered against the royal blue ceiling
  darkness came with a drizzle which burst into torrential down-
pour
          i fell asleep smiling
                         *****

A DAY IN THE MIND (5 ideas dissected in a vignette)

•

the singer on the train track record
is number one in my book
                          while i am zero

i am the sheep
with a bruised blossom
bus ticket
busking knee deep
on highway sixty-one.

i am the pensioner
wearing musky deodorant spray
playing crossword puzzles
on blue foldout pages
of recycle bin salvaged papers.

i am the waterlily
cut with culinary scissors
sold on the street corner
where the coroners daughter
orders her fish & chips parcels.

i am the bingo card
with thirteen odd numbers
never called
in the dusty dartboard
dance hall of the red town square.

i am the rusty harmonica
blowing Memphis anthems
in an overcoat wind
which whistles
stabbing thistle songs.

i am the red raincoat
never worn outside Chelsea hotel
soaked & forgotten
without devotion
of a poet's song.

i am the baptist
fasting with locusts in harsh winter rivers
waiting for a cousin
under pelting stones
with my head on a platter.

i am the seal
starved of oysters
in surrealist poems
& psychedelic beetle
eggmen sing songs.

i am the leper
crawling along cobble stone
pavements
begging for the kingdoms token
in sun stroked delirium.

••

the blue 2D pencil sketched man
lies with his skinny paintbrush hands

chained to bedposts
& scrawny ink-pot legs tied to the tussles
of a dark mustard & oak colored Arabian rug.

the belly of this graphite created graphic
drawn in a dog eared comic book outline
half tattered
the other half plastered with sea shells
& baked root vegetables.

grey scales
of cat and mouse hopscotch
fill the space between his neck and face
in jaw dropping jazz beats
blown in a trombone maze
halting the toe-tapping
tiger-striped finger-click race.

•••

old man at twilight
& the tonsillitis suffered
impressionist portrait
with blurred half blind eyes
as Catalonia sparkles
behind the Raphael worn
stretched ostrich neck.

stern curled upper lip & ebony iris
the tobacco pipe clutched tight in his left hand
is shaded by soft copper portraits
of a window leaning sister.

a neorealistic lady sprawled out
on the rocky beach
displaying geometric diagrams
& golden ratio'd intersections.

in a Virginia garden
with fountains & flowers
a scaffolding tower held his easel
while his canvas draped over the sky.

bird choreographer
shot his backdrops on film
cutting eyes out of cardboard
as surrealism was realized on reel.

••••

Sheepishly the winter kneads
possum breath held tight
in silk woven sacks

we sit in silence watching the scene
unraveling apple seeds seamlessly
as bullet shaped pools breed dust to air
& nightmares disappear under thin wisps.

Saharan palm tree pages
laced with a guitar riff secret
an unveiled wizard gift
of ribbons untied at your feet
as camels bow on ivory padded knees

the glimmer of gold horseshoes
striking light in desert heat.

•••••

skipping through soviet nursery factories
on hums of laughter & checkered shrieks

green & blue
plugged their fingers too
zapped them
i zapped them
their chests went poof

gas pipes drip onto white dressed mystery
pooling under scout socks
& tightly laced military boots
where a sunhat cloaks a beige green rucksack
smack bang in the middle of my Polish panic attack.

ring-a-ring-electricity
pockets filthy & bloody
shocked them
i shocked them
their heads went boom

film reel unwinding the wheel spinning tapes
an auburn haired patient staggers through puddles
where doctors lie twisted rotting in a blood flood.

the moon moves the ocean, hope moves me

i.
I wake up each morning
my mind wrapped around your body.

spiralling in an unbreakable circuit
round and round
bound by terminal planetary rings
orbiting around closed eye film trailers of you
moving through sleeps ghostly shadows
from my pillow, crawling up the wall onto the ceiling
before dropping onto and into me.

watching a candlelight burning in a lighthouse
lantern gallery
the flickering flame, lost to the vast ocean
shines brighter in my bijou room
than the booming, ship seeking torch
striding through darkness in full bloom.

ii.
morning light reflects from strand to cave
shades of sea foam glimmering, dancing on the walls
along with the sharp silver glint of abalone shell calls
jellyfish breaking through alabaster spume waves
while the ocean orchestra bellows your name...

in and out as the tide marches against the shore
under the eye of a soft seine sunrise
to the strokes of a setting stella d'oro sunset

and waning to waxing, new through to full
the moonlight and brightness of day, shine your name...

iii.
under the starlit ceiling
i swim in harp string lullabies
swaying across the sky
diving into the sea
where saints go to die

       in the ocean of time
life is better when i close my eyes.

une immense espoir a traversé l'océan
une immense espérance a traversé la terre

paradise is a beach ball floating on waves in silence

/
serving in a squash match of philosophy
set on the Garden Route forest court
on the East Coast
        i bounce my brain
off of the spekboom trees.
a treaty sealed in a binocular nod
with two woodpeckers perched on a yellowwood.
            they lend me their wings & bird eyes
opening the dome sky window of flight above
                                the woods
opening the lids to see the toxicity of the city.

in that forest
i burnt my dress shoes & ripped skinny jeans
                on square pegs in flames.
laying the walkway on the blue printed path
leading to interstellar epsom salt baths
& crystal pools of untapped tonic
brewed by aligned stars on comet tails
running to overflow my skull shaped mug.

//
out of the dark
        my footprints
            are light beacons
& scattered bread crumbs
feed me tokens

more precious than gold
building blocks for a launchpad into tomorrow
　　　　　　　　　~ of no cash value ~
　　to penguin suit
　　single lane
　　blinkered merchants
　　　　　　who sell lies over the phone
along backward roads
　　loading their faulted vaults in hollow halls
　　stacked with museum treasures
　　hidden in blood stained endeavours.

　　///
crooked spines build skyscrapers
　　　　　　　　　　out of bones
following babel inspired ambitions
　　spotted with chemically laced
eye socket visions & parasitical
　　　　　　stock market ventures

　　　　　　　　　my feet dangle off the edge
while i lie on the flying board plank
gazing into the shut eye kingdoms
　　beyond chiropractor hammers
　　　　seeing the faces of kings
who transcended flesh & death
　　to earn god crowned eternal
　　　　　　statue status.

　　////
paradise is a beach ball
floating on
　　　　　waves in *silence*
while cosmic explosions
erode the shackles of mortal definitions.

the fall (one size fits all)

Ce monde me réduit à rien. Cela me porte jusqu'au bout. Sans
colère, il nie que j'existe. Et, acceptant ma défaite, je me dirige
vers une sagesse où tout a déjà été conquis - sauf que les larmes
me viennent aux yeux, et ce grand sanglot de poésie qui me
gonfle le cœur me fait oublier la vérité du monde

we exist in a black & white world
where they burn your flag & your pride
if you stray outside the confining outlines

loose cannon jazz leads to blue looks
for swimming upstream to birth cool
in a pace which rips through rule books

black sheep are shot for grazing at night
in a fight against driftwood wearing hoods
instead of uniform peaks, woven in lilywhite

snowflakes aim to form a synchronized shape
& euthanize, medicate & lobotomize
Houdini's who break or partake in a chain escape

led by lego brick leaders
stacked thick in piles of dimes a dozen
fed stacks to build a kingdom for the one

throw your TV's through the window of possibilities
& step outside the jars of clay
spinning in the hands of potters plotting a payday by foul-play

follow brave men down the road not taken
where the grass is greener & the air is cleaner
for the paved path ends at a kool-aid drinking fountain.

Restore the factory settings of my heart

Eight thousand puzzle-piece
butterflies
fill the memory carded banks
of discarded blank
cyberspace Alzheimers.

An empty room with silhouetted views,
creating illusion imitating
hallucinations
of a promise to reinstall the words lost
to safety proof
false parachutes.

Without canvas-sized,
indestructible evidence
or ink-based remembrance -
only erasable by flames,
flood or
unsigned credentials
fallen hand in glove
into
overenthusiastic forgetfulness.

there remains to be seen
a virus immune to tonic,
vaccine,
or innocent naive dreams
capable of murdering,
erasing,

and deleting every letter
conceived by keyboard finger-fucking.

Here sits a love sick junkie
with his head in the clouds
which would rain purple-hazed
words on the handful around;
those who remain concrete laced
flat on the ground in silence
while the sky promises rain -
yet only delivers clouds thundering sounds
of yesterday's romantic morose cries.

The dreams and visions of publicized ambition
dead
to files of hard-drive suicide -
by pornographic escapism,
prism-shaped with temporary reflection
of a soul due to expire.
Teadless and tired
in need of eternal service with supervision
by technology and savvy technicians -
mechanics of the afterlife,
while sighs of a Leonard Cohen existence
drown out the cries
of a bad cup of immortality.

Red-eyed mornings with deleted history
control-shift-n
and go go incognito
of a different kind.
free of decision or any conscious mind -
without a driver at the wheel

deciding the turns,
for any burning yearning sensation to stay,
go, hop-off and arrive.

The destination won't be seen alive.
Even as stains of lead will remain after death
with every orchestrated fable and tale
told by its grey-eyed author immortal,
while multidimensional gurus of ancient fires have stories and
songs
done wrong by sins
of broken-telephone
though burning in hearts, souls,
and every orifice available to spark -
still end up with the scent of unholy shit.

The blank void of all memory is all that remains
throughout every special momentous occasion with hard-copy
refection
or recollection of that holy time and spiritual place -
I await judgement and punishment
or divine rejection,
for falling in love and forgetting to save.

life is beautiful

i would fall from heights
shaking Lucifer terrified
for Luna's starry skies to linger,
in a Jashar night, by your side.

floating on Chopin stroked ivory nocturnes
swimming in deep ruby pools of Pinot Noir
dancing on your flowering lips,
sweet with vanilla cigarette smoke.

life is beautiful.

phosphorus waves of purple patches
carry me from seas of stormy eyes
onto shores sanctuary with blue skies
harbored in your sheltering arms.

brighter than painted pages
singing lullabies in the city of angels,
blinded dizzy by the light shining
through the iris of your eyes.

life is beautiful.

punctured bicycle on a hillside
spread by skyscraper flames
burning my humble log cabin existence
halcyon falls to ash on the ground.

chopped mountaintop forest
crumbling down to street corners
begging for coins or breadcrumbs
and bleeding on pavements in darkness.

life is dreadful.

burst dam walls of crippling cancer
flow from drowning depths of hell
crashing high waters
washing away life's short circuit (un)certainty.

reading Dante at your bedside grave,
flowers lie dead on tombstones
spread in autumns cemetery
as you lay where i may never go.

life is dreadful.

www.ingramcontent.com/pod-product-compliance
Lightning Source LLC
LaVergne TN
LVHW051459170726
843492LV00002B/722